Motherhood

QUOTES FROM AND ABOUT MOTHERS

Edited by
Leslie Carola

Longmeadow Press

*T*hanks, Mom, for being my mom, my friend,
and the best teacher anybody could ever have.

Janet Dailey

*W*ith four kids you can forget about order: you just have to hope you don't crack your ankles stumbling over three bags of marbles and a Tinker Toy.

Betty Ford

*T*he darn trouble with cleaning the house is it gets dirty the next day anyway, so skip a week if you have to. The children are the most important thing.

Barbara Bush

*T*he little things that I never really noticed all come back now as I have my own daughter. Thanks, Mom, for being such a strong model for me. You made it seem easy.

Meredith Ralston

*I*t was my mother who taught us to stand up to our problems, not only in the world around us but in ourselves.

Dorothy Pitman Hughes

*I*t's the three pair of eyes that mothers have to have....One pair that see through closed doors. Another in the back of her head... and, of course, the ones in front that can look at a child when he goofs up and reflect 'I understand and I love you' without so much as uttering a word.

Erma Bombeck

*M*other is the name for God in the lips and hearts of children.

W. M. Thackery

*W*ho ran to help me when I fell,
And would some pretty story tell,
or kiss the place to make it well?
My mother.

Ann Taylor

*I*f I were damned of body and soul,
I know whose prayers would make me whole,
Mother o' mine, O mother o' mine.

Rudyard Kipling

A mother is not a person to lean on but a person to make leaning unnecessary.

Dorothy Canfield Fisher

*N*o matter how old a mother is she watches her middle-aged children for signs of improvement.

Florida Scott-Maxwell

*T*hat lovely voice; how I should weep for joy if I could hear it now!

Colette

*W*hat **do** girls do who haven't any mothers to help them through their troubles?

Louisa May Alcott

*A*h lucky girls who grow up in the shelter of a mother's love — a mother who knows how to ...take advantage of propinquity without allowing appetites to be dulled by habit.

Edith Wharton

*I*s not a young mother one of the sweetest sights life shows us?

William Makepeace Thackery

*W*omen know the way to rear up children...
They know a simple, merry, tender knack
Of tying sashes, fitting baby-shoes,
And stringing pretty words that make no
sense....

Elizabeth Barrett Browning

*S*ome are kissing mothers and some are scolding
mothers, but it is love just the same, and most
mothers kiss and scold together.

Pearl S. Buck

*W*e bear the world, and we make it....There was never a great man who had not a great mother — it is hardly an exageration.

Olive Schreiner

*M*ost mothers are instinctive philosophers.

Harriet Beecher Stowe

*T*he commonest fallacy among women is that simply having children makes one a mother — which is as absurd as believing that having a piano makes one a musician.

S. J. Harris

*O*ne race there is of men, one of gods, but from one mother we both draw our breath.

Pindar

*C*hildren find comfort in flaws, ignorance, insecurities similar to their own. I love my mother for letting me see hers.

Erma Bombeck

*T*he real secret behind motherhood...love, the thing that money can't buy. Show your children that you really and truly love them.

Anna Crosby

*S*o for the mother's sake the child was dear,
And dearer was the mother for the child.

Coleridge

*G*od knows that a mother needs fortitude and
courage and tolerance and flexibility and
patience and firmness and nearly every other brave
aspect of the human soul.

Phyllis McGinley

M ost of us have learned that there is not even
a semblance of a replacement for that vital
potion we call 'mother love,' be it from a biological
parent or a special someone who mothers us along the
way.

Melissa Hartman

M en are what their mothers made them.

Ralph Waldo Emerson

I cannot bear a mother's tears.

Virgil

A child without a mother is like a door
without a doorknob.

A mother understands what a child does not say.

One mother achieves more than a hundred teachers.

The warmest bed of all is mother's.

The best fork is mother's hand.

God could not be everywhere, so He made mothers.

Yiddish proverbs

A lways remember that your *son is going to grow up to be* somebody else's *husband.*

Fran Wright

A mother's children are like ideas;
none are as wonderful as her own.

Chinese fortune

A suburban mother's role is to deliver children obstetrically once, and by car for ever after.

Peter de Vries

B y and large, mothers and housewives are the only workers who do not have regular time off. They are the great vacationless class.

Madeleine L'Engle

*T*he more people have studied different methods
of bringing up children the more they have
come to the conclusion that what good mothers and
fathers instinctively feel like doing for their babies is
the best after all.

Benjamin Spock

*M*other knows best.

Edna Ferber

I didn't realize how much I would learn from my children. They have shown me there are more important things than planning and organizing. They've given me more humanity.

Joanna Quillen

*C*hildren reinvent your world for you.

Susan Sarandon

I saw a cradle at a cottage door,
Where the fair mother, with her cheerful wheel,
Carolled so sweet a song, that the young bird
Which, timid, near the threshold sought for
seeds,
Paused on its lifted foot, and raised its head,
As if to listen.

  Lydia Howard Sigourney

*M*y son will never realize how much I learned from him .... He gave me more insight into how to deal with children than anyone; for that I thank and love him.

Pearl Bailey

*M*om is a tough friend. I know she is going to be honest with me.

Robert Eldridge

*M*y priorities have always been the family.
That's where I sprout from. That's where
my happiness is. If I'm not happy there, other
things don't help. I like that grounding.

Goldie Hawn

*P*erhaps a better woman after all,
With chubby children hanging on my neck
To keep me low and wise.

Elizabeth Barrett Browning

*M*others have to handle all kinds of situations. When presented with the new baby brother he said he wanted, the toddler told his mother ''I changed my mind.''

Judith Viorst

*R*aising children is far more creative than most jobs around for men and women.

Benjamin Spock

S he who had cared for me day in, day out
during my childhood, driving me here and
there, soothed me when I was hurt, worried with
me over problems, and set me an example of poise,
courage, and gallantry.

Molly Haskin

M y mother taught me to walk proud and tall
'as if the world was mine.' I remember that
line, and I think it brought me some luck.

Sophia Loren

M y mother's best advice to me was: "Whatever you decide to do in life, be sure that the joy of doing it does not depend upon the applause of others, because in the long run we are, all of us, alone."

Ali MacGraw

S he always tried to impress upon me the importance of treating everybody as you want to be treated.

Albert Bethune on mother
Dr. Mary McL. Bethune

*F*urnish an example, stop preaching, stop shielding, don't prevent self-reliance and initiative, allow your children to develop along their own lines.

Eleanor Roosevelt

*T*he best advice from my mother was a reminder to tell my children everyday: ''Remember you are loved.''

Evelyn McCormick

*M*y mother is drawn to need and the sweetness of the needy....My warmest memories of my mother are from times when I was sick, or in pain, or in some kind of trouble.

Susan Cheever

*H*er children rise up and call her blessed.

Proverbs

*I*t goes without saying, you should never have more children than you have car windows.

Erma Bombeck

*I*n the beginning, you're hoping for a blond or a girl or a violin prodigy, but when you realize your time has come, all you do is pray for a normal, healthy baby.

Betty Ford

I *begin to love this little creature, and to anticipate his birth as a fresh twist to a knot, which I do not wish to untie.*

Mary Wollstonecraft

S *uddenly she was here. And I was no longer pregnant; I was a mother. I never believed in miracles before.*

Ellen Greene

*F*rom the instant I saw her, a tiny red creature bathed in the weird underwater light of the hospital operating room, I loved her with an intensity that life had not prepared me for.

Susan Cheever

*H*ow could I explain the enormous feeling of security in knowing that now she was with me in the world?...We would discusss everything in life... and help each other be real people.

Liv Ullmann

A t the maternity home they entered into her medical record:''Weight...3 kilograms 100 grams. A healthy child.'' I remember that entry by heart: in those happy days the words were music to my ears.

Raisa Gorbachev

I n the sheltered simplicity of the first days after a baby is born, one sees again the magical closed circle, the miraculous sense of two people existing only for each other.

Anne Morrow Lindbergh

*T*hen someone placed her in my arms. She looked up at me. The crying stopped. Her eyes melted through me, forging a connection in me with their soft heat.

Shirley MacLaine

*T*he most amazing moment was when he was handed to me in his little blanket, and looked at me with his huge blue eyes.

Margaret Drabble

I looked at this tiny, perfect creature and it was as though a light switch had been turned on. A great rush of love, mother love, flooded out of me.

Madeleine L'Engle

*I*t is a feeling of intimacy and exclusiveness.... a warm, lazy intimate gaiety. I feel...a need to laugh out in triumph, because of this marvelous, precarious, immortal human being.

Doris Lessing

I had a baby. He was beautiful and mine. Totally mine. No one had bought him for me.

Maya Angelou

*A*nd he gave us a little baby. A little baby to love. I am so glad.

Tillie Olson

No event ever in my life has been so profound, so joyful, so moving. I fell in love as I never have before or since.

Ali MacGraw

It's such a powerful connection; it takes me by surprise. I feel like there's a dotted line connecting me to my son.

Sarah Langston

I love being a mother. I am more aware. I feel things on a deeper level. I seem to have more of everything now: more love, more magic, more energy.

Shelley Long

*W*hen you are a mother, you are never really alone in your thoughts. You are connected to your child and to all those who touch your lives. A mother always has to think twice, once for herself and once for her child.

Sophia Loren

I *n the evening, after she has gone to sleep, I kneel beside the crib and touch her face, where it is pressed against the slats, with mine.*

Joan Didion

S *tep motherhood was so joyous that it was responsible for my decision to have a child.*

Candace Bergen

*H*ow I love her lusty laugh. It brings the sunshine in, and echoes through my day.

Liza Barry

*T*o be accurate about it, I was nuts about my baby. I couldn't wait to get her up in the morning just to see what she would do.

Beverly Sills

*T*here is nothing more absorbing than a baby, nothing more intoxicating.

*I*t is impossible for me to believe that anything I write could have a fraction of the importance of the child growing inside me....

Mary Gordon

*W*here else is love that pure?

Susan Connors

*T*he things that used to be important to me
aren't any more. Work is not that important. I
love what I do but it never takes precedence over what
is good for them [the children] and our marriage.

Debby Boone

*T*here is no place in the world I would rather be
than home with my child.

Anna Fisher

I would like to be the perfect mom, the perfect wife and the perfect golfer. But I've found that's almost impossible.

Nancy Lopez

B eing a mother makes me feel as if I got my membership in an exclusive club.

Andie MacDowell

I love his laugh,....it bubbles out in an infectious wholehearted way. This is pure joy — nothing else matters.

Anne Morrow Lindbergh

E very little minute matters....Maybe I feel this way because I waited so long to have a child.

Jaclyn Smith

I *found such pleasure in the simple, everyday*
things: a walk around the block, just getting out-
side each day, collecting leaves or seashells or pebbles ,
or picking flowers in the garden.

Eileen Lawton

I *'ve gained a great feeling of peace from being a*
mother....The ability to love is the heart of the
matter.

Gloria Vanderbilt

*T*he great high of winning Wimbledon lasts for about a week....But having a baby — there just isn't any comparison!

Chris Evert

*T*he love I feel for my child is like a balloon that keeps filling up and expanding. It never bursts, it just keeps getting bigger and bigger. Maybe, over a lifetime, the love will fill many balloons!

Judy Schmidt

I've always felt I've had luck, certainly in obvious areas. And now I have the greatest blessing of all — these children.

What would I want engraved on my gravestone for posterity? "Mother."

Jessica Lange

You have a child, and you can't be a perfectionist anymore.

Mary Beth Hurt

I have three great children. I realize how fast
childhood goes, ...so I cherish it that much more.

Sally Field

*N*ow that I have these children, I'm just crazed
about the world's making it to the next
century.

Meryl Streep

I t's the little things you do day in and day out that
count. That's the way you teach your children.

Amanda Pays

L oving a child doesn't mean giving in to all his
whims; to love him is to bring out the best in
him, to teach him to love what is difficult.

Nadia Boulanger

*S*ome people make work their personal life, but I chose to have a family. That's my career.

Mia Farrow

*S*inging to the children inspired me, and I am still influenced by their tastes.

Carly Simon

I just couldn't live without children....
Motherhood has relaxed me in many ways. I've
become a juggler, I suppose. It's all a big circus.

Jane Seymour

For a woman, a son offers the best chance to
know the mysterious male existence.

Carole Klein

*A*nnie's brought me an incredible amount of sensitivity, and ... she's made me a nicer person.

Glenn Close

*M*y darling little girl-child, after such a long and troublesome waiting I now have you in my arms. I am alone no more. I have my baby.

Martha Martin

*O*ur first mother-daughter outing: For three hours, knitting our thoughts and lives together like old college roommates going toward a reunion.

Phyllis Theroux

*T*hou art thy mother's glass, and she in thee Calls back the lovely April of her prime.

William Shakespeare

I'm sorry you are wiser,
I'm sorry you are taller;
I liked you better foolish,
And I liked you better smaller.

Aline Kilmer

*I*n the eyes of its mother every beetle is a gazelle.

Moroccan proverb

I long to put the experience of fifty years at once into your young lives, to give you at once the key of that treasure chamber every gem of which has cost me tears and struggles and prayers, but you must work for these inward treasures yourselves.

Harriet Beecher Stowe

*D*ear Mother: I'm all right. Stop worrying about me.

Egyptian Papyrus letter c. 2000 BC

*O*h, Mama, just look at me one minute as though you really saw me....Let's look at one another....It goes so fast. We don't have time to look at one another....Do any human beings ever realize life while they live it — every, every minute?

> *Emily Webb from Thornton Wilder's* Our Town.